SHE CARRIES THE SWORD

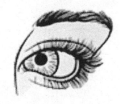

CHEYENNA CLEARBROOK

the pain you carry is valid
it shields you
let it go

I struggle with old friend- pain,
it tells me to write
how can I help?
pour it out

I am thankful to my friends and family members who have led me out of my darkness and into my light.

They, and you, are dedicated to this poetry book.

I understand that it's difficult to believe you're alone, but you're not alone. I am with you. We are all.

The light is inside you, take it out and shine brilliantly.

It can be hard for you to keep fighting your demons every second, minute, hour, and day, but you are winning again.

You keep winning, we're cheering for you and your demons will be conquered. I'm still fighting with my demons, which means we're fighting together.

contents

THE LONELINESS

my heart is getting cold.
colder, then colder
as if it had been abandoned to
a hot one,
I'm tired of myself

am I really lost
wandering about, wandering
yelling and still crying
no one has heard my limitless cries though,
I am lonely,
drowning inside
no one is coming just
I'm dying of my isolation,
for the very last time and for the very last time, I yelled
the very last breath I take is

when the isolation emerges
you're drowning
in
a heap of shadows
the hopeless need for yourself

and why are you so cruel
aches in my body
and you like them like you,
I'm falling

you have taken me for granted,
I have given you too much.
you are crushing the spirit of my
all that you left me, only pain
I feel so broken,
like a shattered doll

many of the kindest persons
the lonely people are,
when shooting a burned star
a last look at elegance
granting sad wishes to those
who want
to see
but it's made to fire alone,

in these tears, it comes down on me
being apart from my mind's soul
from the bottom of the ocean
into the sun,
yet it climbs into hell
leaving only agony inside,
unleash demons
I have fallen

I've been trying to breathe in,
a breath that is as big as the sun
and my lungs, but inside me,
there is a hollow
when something collapses on you,
 it is hard to breathe.
expanding
to the world, to the astonishing line
between reality and
my demons swelled,
there is not enough space to
breathe in
like I'm lying down
eternity waiting
not even a breath that is as heavy
as the sun

I kept finding myself anxious.
I was bored of those little stuff.
it is impossible to focus.
when you are feeling alone,
It started to drag me into it.
and deeper, deeper,
all remains alone,

when a time machine exists,
I'd do it all in a heartbeat,
not to feel something
in the bubble, curling up
it saves me from being
undetached thoughts have driven me to
to have a sense of security

I walk any time I go.
behind me, the shadow is trailing
when I'm with humans,
though it's dark,

a void, a space filled with darkness
it feels good, eats me up, eats me up...
I try to fake and hide my darkness,
jokes, all the smiles, the chats, the talks

it is isolated, lonely,
the darkness I can't stop,

my dreams, ambitions, enjoyment
stopped the flow
I feel so alone, so alone,
I don't have much else to share, and
how can I find a light here?
to shine on the
when I have lost all faith
people have deserted me
my family ones, my mates
nobody sees me now.
I am lonely

I love the emptiness
but I hate feeling empty
being too numb
I got lost

at night
chaos becomes everything.
my mind went wild.
the crawl of my demons
it's making me scream,

it yells,
make fun of me
I shut my eyes and
 I close my eyes and
hoping for it to go down

it didn't, but
this teases me,
having lost myself

onto the mound of darkness that
I can't go back to

my demons enjoy
certain nights of sleeplessness,
I have lost my virginity to the dark,

where the light is,

THE PAIN

both the tears,
it causes more discomfort.
losing a bit of the facts
gaining the sense of numbness
words are words
it does not have to be published,
in my head, it is all over.

what is real
what is not real

I have lost the sense of
realizing if
is everything real
or some sort of delusion inside
my head,
who am I
am I real

it was pure passion, all love...
it was just hate.
and this for the heart of a heart,
all this hurt a lot.
all the pain inside of me
all of all
all I had is investing
that now feels like worthlessness

are you tired of that?
binding the confusion
within you and stuck
back and forward
not realizing where
you're standing
all this war, all this battle,
becomes obsolete
all you feel was defensive,

all eyes on me
to judge of hate
growing pain inside me
the eyes continue to
be seen on me
I am drowning
my heartaches
I'm forgetting my pain
I'm feeling numb

the unceasing fight
the sense in isolation
what eyes are on me
the ambient chill
I've been losing the sense of
reality
I lost.

obsessed, you are
but it just hurt me
why do you do that
why do you want to do it
pulling me to be tormented
why are you hanging around
it's killing me
why do you think that hitting me
is okay
you left me, however the agony of
my trauma

I am numb
I can't tell whether it will cure or kill me
I am tired of myself
I just fought and fighting
I am becoming weaker and weaker
the light that is dying inside me
I want to sleep
forever

I was trying to search it,
there is no sun, but
it was everything, in the end,
the darkness
awaits for me

your eyes are focused on my naked core
filled with envy
wrathful inside of you
it's smoking me
throwing stones at you
shattering me
I lost a war
your drifting gaze
the other soul

I heard all bitterly loud words of me
it makes no difference
yet I have listened to your words
it all shatters
I befall

I was your mistake, I was
I have given you all
your heart was my heart
the goodness which I have given you
my time has been granted to you,
I have been your worth
you are abandoning me
you were playing with me
you left me so I left you but,
the pains I'm wearing
I'm unloved

pain is my drug
it is addicting
to release
in the cosmos losing myself
became my best friend
only one
understand me

the pain is real
it holds me close
the feeling of being numb
yeah, 24/7

I feel safe
pretending to pretend
hide from the sun, hide from myself

THE STRENGTH

it takes resilience

to reminisce amiably

the cruel standing

some people
fill with hatred
to them
you must be a light
to shine on

the greatest tragedy when

you lost yourself

is to build

rise yourself

shake your grounds

rise yourself

you are you
you are loved
you are inspired
you are still
you are your soulmate

to protect my heart, I don't need you to
or should the hole in me be filled with
on my own, I want to be complete.
I need me to feed my love to fill it with my love
the *void*
I just light my heart with light,
not you,

I am the writer of my narrative,
the flaw you are looking for
in my story, you're trying to kill
you suppose I was the opportunity
for you,
the black ink in my veins runs,
you think that you're going
to tear my sheet of paper,
the unworthy of you
I had you stuck in my chalk,
you need not flee,
you're caught up in my story,
you are a beast
I am the editor,
just me, just

as she said, holding me in her arms
think of the one thing
what is one thing holds you back
your fear
they will attack you
drowning in the water
losing yourself
you must rise
you must overcome
stomp over the grounds
your fear be below

like a river flowing into me, I found calm.
for so long, it pulled me out...
stuck in the ocean
floating about, floating

I had my water stand still and
eventually relaxed,

you've been learning how to ascend,
you went for those hard barriers,
through,
you did it and it is your triumph.
wearing the best stance you have,
see the worst moments
how many times have you rolled over
but and,
you're on top of the majestic mountains here

they say bravery is courage.
and you've all got to be,
mounting needs a lot of power to

you could be fragile because it needs
a great deal of willpower to open your eyes
and to be open wide

only you wield your power,
finding light
through the mastery of your soul

and now the universe has found your light
now,
the message that comes from your strength
in inner force

spreading that light

THE ME

I am the maker of a mind of my own
I am the controller of dreams of my own
I am the predator of desires of my own,
I am the leader of my heart
I am the listener with words of my own
I am the anchor to my own emotions.

I look at me and cry
I wipe my tears
everything hurts
I remain smile
I am strong
I am going to be okay

I have lost all
everything
and I am still here
walking with my ambition
I remain strong

why do you want to
when you feel down,
when the world has turned against you
you have no idea what to do.
it sheds tears
it's blowing backwards
you are lost,

when the night sky hides the moon,
it's not going to glow
like stars
listening to you...

over your head,
when life is a dream,
then you dread yourself,
why do you want to

when the world seems to be perfect,
where is your contentment and gentleness?
you ask yourself why, then

let me be poetry
write down my fears
erase all traumas
but remember them
telling me
how to find my strength
my bravery
and I began editing
the black ink that is washed off
replaced with artistic words

I deserve to have my love,
I am loved, loved,
nobody claims that I'm not loved.
I deserve to be more than this.
not fewer, not less than
I'm worth every penny,
in me, I see

when night comes
I'm seeing the stars
it's all breezing,
I could feel coldness,
I'm lying back
glancing at the stars
I'm curious about stars
they're moving me
through a state of gratitude
that leaves me wondering,
perplexing the world
in my chest and lumps of
 sensation in my throat

I need to become a star
shooting away
be free
becoming one with the universe

my mind's weight
engraved on my body
eyes that are sitting on mine
harmonize heartbeats
in choreography, I fell

I've been laying my head on the pillow
I've been tangling my body and curling
like the desire to expand, my eyes
started to drift
heartbeats are increasingly being
there are flowing visions
in the head of me

I have been dancing for years.
till I wake up

I've seen myself
in the ball of crystal
of all that,

and vowed, and
still flowing through to be
none of that, all of that,

it has to pass through

and then they heard,
a bell is ringing

I found an old photograph.
I see me,
smiling
taking the lane of memory within my brain
recalling
all of the suffering, joy, and satisfaction
the hours, those moments
I recalled that,
this has taken me to today
with all those memories that I have made,

my entire life has been written in chapters of
dusting through the bookshelves
from the outset
this remains unclear to the end, but
each word has a story.
under these narratives,
it either haunts or times of pleasure
each chapter is a lesson

if I had
just fallen asleep,
what's going to
happen to my soul?
unconscious being
I'm going
to forget
vanishing into
thin air
I am terrified
of falling asleep.
I would
like to know,
I want to sit awake,
and I want to
my soul must
be on fire.
not diming

one day,
I wake up and,
realizing I matter
not the world or you,
to myself

I matter.

when I'm falling apart
I'm sewing myself
each inch of the string
stitching,
to get the gap filled
whenever I get hurt,
I'm sewing
all of it

everything I have is me, everything I have
towards the end of the day
I get me,
I don't need to take someone with me
but me

THE YOU

like the sand of time, your skin is like
your eyes are as blue as the ocean.
like the rose that flower, the lips are just like
your smile is so crazy all the time.
you are beautiful.

I'm the one waiting for you most,
the soul of emptiness
I see you only as a living form,
you are a living soul, and you are
I long for your soul

you spit a fire
spread rapidly
continue on
you close your eyes
the fire fades away
you feel calm

you close your eyes
you see the darkness
when you open your eyes
there is a light
reach that light
hold that tightly

I need you
the warmth of yours
that illuminates my soul,
my soul spills out,
other than you,
it is so complicated.
I want you

the lips of yours
I desire to,
I miss you

if you got all the thunder summoned,
lighting all over the room
overpowering you inside
take charge of your thunder,
it gave you the power to represent on,

thunder, be thunder
strike an ignition

you don't have to worry then,
and what you were able to do
moving along

deep down inside of you
you knew, you did,
you have to go deep into the
take out all your troubles from your tongue

difficulties lead you on,
this savours you,
disturbing you

you remember, shake it off, you know,
take out the garbage for them
the one that handed it on to you,
my dear
meet the within you
you know, you do,

pull the troubles out

THE LOVE

two souls entwined in the light
goes against the darkness
a new love blooms
they became one

your departure taught me
how to be a herb
where I'm watering my seeds
I realize that I don't need you
I need my roses, so I need them

what I thought was passion.
what I thought was love.
you have shown me the fullness of love.
I am aware about you,
all the material
it reminds me that I have
if you hit me again, it doesn't matter.
I do think you are stunning.
your weaknesses, not
just you, just you,
I am trapped
grasping around in your fingers

where is your touch
your burning body's warmth
I'm craving
pumps for the pulse
when I touch you
your heartbeat rises
your touch is responsive
wrapping with your fingers
tightly
I can't let go of you

your love for me is poisonous.
swiftly spreading
it eats me up because,
I would have done anything but for you,
you're using me
I didn't care
everything I wanted was to be loved.
it's blinding me
I've been losing myself
attaching intensely to you
deep down in you
you're craving,
you loved this, you have

I was losing myself to you

betraying me all over once again
I was so used to that,
I have forgotten what it takes to be in love.
all I tasted was toxic.
it kills me,
what love is like
I got lost
with or was it delusion with your passion
I'm too excited to
for love of yours
your love and affection
yet I knew that,
it's bad for me, like

your aroma is nuts.
sweet as honey
makes me unconscious
floating and dreaming
through the hole in the black,
I have seen you
in a fantasy of mine,
I am attracted to you
it's got to be a fantasy, but
your presence can be sensed by me
having kissed my naked skin
my skin's chilling
I'm moaning

you are real, but you are

or was it all my dream

I can't tell which

let's float together
into the galaxy
just two of us
against the universe

you and me

piercing your aura into me
at that time, I died.
when you walk through a room,
t's all spinning
am I dying
I'm so dizzy.
you are so toxic that you are
we're able to mix together,
my chemical burns
you fire, you burn.

I want you,
Your body isn't
the aura of yours
soul of yours
I want that

your taste is so intoxicating,
I'm losing myself
 to you
I am yours,
neverending

my body yearns for you,
the lip of your
 your hair
the eyes of your

everything about you
intoxicating is
I am addicted
your touch makes me shiver.
 like ice,
you are in flames,

SHE

she alone can light her soul
the soul inside her
is flaming
it seeks her
she alone will pierce her soul
just her

she is very resilient
the only thing she can alter is her mindset
of the own her
and a warrior
she became these that
too more or less
she yet walks above her but,
her crown awaits
she is you

she's not me
her character is not mine
the definition of her attractiveness
s not my definition
I am not she, I am not her
I am me
my personality belongs to me
I am gorgeous

she is hurt
yet held her tears
the pain swept through
her heart is already broken
yet she was walking
her smile covers her pain
yet she held her past
she's got the whole story
concealed in yet
she needs to yell
bur her pain is holding her down
she needs it to be let go
yet she is afraid

she was rare
I have missed her
only she can just open my eyes
I wounded her there,
she would be never compared
with other women
I lost her
she was my anchor
I was driving her away
she won, and
I let her go
it seems she is happy
it pains me
to see her going on
I do love her so much
she was the one who got away
all I had her was a dream of her

she is the poem
the description of her walking is that of
a soul that is alive
words ought not to be described as
she is infinity, infinity
with her, no words can be compared.

no one can claims her
her mindset
no one can replace her with others
her kindness
no one can dim her light
her light
only she can claims hers

she is the galaxy
sun is her light and
mercury is her thoughts
venus is her infectious
earth is her growth
moon is her energy
mars is her beauty
juptier is her love
saturn is her power
uranus is her strength
neptune is her anchor
pluto is her defender
she is you

she didn't talk about how desperate she is at all
when she said that she was
and get her dead ends sealed off
not to extend,
letting go of it

if she was born with weakness,
to collapse

but you were *blessed* with the potential to rise with
your power.

don't keep it back for a moment,
don't just be like her, don't
be you,
only you can

they said that it was empty
but she said,
there is room
it attracts her that way

that room is her sun, her light.
shining brilliantly before them
much more,
that overcomes everything that goes in her path.

she is a silent fighter with her demons,
struggling to breathe freely
that stole her bright light from her
but
she knows that she can *overcome*
the monsters inside her
she is the one holding the sword
to slay her demons
she is her victory

your triumph is yours
victory belongs to you all

in your story, you are the winner
not theirs
your demons are not
not the endless fights

not till later

Made in the USA
Monee, IL
21 January 2021